Bob Dylan's Career as a Blakean Visionary and Romantic

by Eugene Stelzig

Milne Library
Geneseo, NY

2013

©①◎ 2013 Eugene Stelzig
This work is licensed under a [Creative Commons Attribution-ShareAlike 3.0 Unported License](#).

Published by Milne Library, State University of New York at Geneseo, Geneseo, NY 14454

Cover image by Rowland Scherman accessed through the National Archives and Records Administration at http://research.archives.gov/description/542021. This work is in the public domain in the United States because it is a work of the United States Federal Government under the terms of 17 U.S.C. § 105

Cover and book design by Allison P. Brown

PREFACE

"Bob Dylan's Career as a Blakean Visionary and Romantic" was completed in 1976 as an invited contribution to a volume of academic and scholarly essays on Dylan to be published by the Popular Press and edited by Patrick Morrow. After the volume was accepted and the publication contract was signed, the Popular Press reneged on the agreement, apparently because it felt the volume would fall between the cracks: Dylan's popular fan base would not be interested in a book of academic articles, and academics would not be interested in a pop culture idol. Obviously things have changed considerably in the intervening decades!

Robert Shelton contacted me when he was writing his biographical study, *No Direction Home: The Life and Music of Bob Dylan* (1986), to request a copy of my essay. He quotes from it several times in the book, but in the Bibliography (mis)identifies it as an "unpublished dissertation, date unknown." Over the years I have had a number of requests for copies of my article, mostly from graduate students writing dissertations on Dylan, and more recently from a faculty member teaching a course on Blake and Dylan.

My discussion—almost four decades ago—of the deep affinities between Dylan's song poetry and the Romantics, especially William Blake, is one of the early "scholarly" as opposed to popular appreciations of Dylan's art and his oeuvre from his first album up to and including *Desire* (1976).

I wish to thank Paul Schacht, Chair of SUNY Geneseo's English Department, for suggesting that Geneseo's Milne Library make "Bob Dylan's Career as a Blakean Visionary and Romantic" available both online and in print, as well as Cyril Oberlander, Director of SUNY Geneseo's Milne Library, and his staff for following through on this suggestion.

Eugene Stelzig
SUNY Distinguished Teaching Professor of English

I know that This World
Is a World of Imagination & Vision.

Blake

I

That Bill's a foolish fellow
He has given me a black eye
He does not know how to handle a bat
Any more than a dog or a cat
He has knocked down the wicket
And broke the stumps
And runs without shoes to save his pumps

These lines could be in a Dylan song and not seem particularly out of place: the absurd subject matter, presented in an offhand but rather break-neck conversational manner that embraces the ungrammatical ("has broke the stumps"), coupled with a reliance on simple rhymes that impart to the whole a light-hearted, limericky quality, is characteristic of a certain kind of Dylan lyric. One thinks of an impromptu satirico-absurd piece like "Tombstone Blues," where the speaker wishes he "could give brother Bill his great thrill" and chain him on top of—what?—naturally, a hill. The stanza above is not by Dylan ("wicket" and "pumps" are the disqualifiers), but by the early and then almost totally-unknown William Blake, writing nearly two hundred years ago in his satire, *An Island in the Moon*. Such striking convergences between the poetry of Blake and that of Dylan could be multiplied, but, by way of counterpoint, I will let a quotation from Dylan in his apocryphal mode that invites a parallel quotation from Blake suffice as one instance of a larger pattern of fairly obvious resemblances: "Are birds free from the chains of the skyway?" asks the bard of "Ballad in Plain D" most "mysteriously" at the end of his lament. And Blake, at the end of the first "Memorable Fancy" of *The Marriage of Heaven and Hell*, leaves us with the cryptic question, "How do you know but ev'ry Bird that cuts the airy way, / Is an immense world of delight clos'd by your senses five?"

What I have signaled so far is mostly a matter of manner, the sort of similarity between two writers that, for apparent reasons, invites critical notice but hardly repays study. All that glitters is not often all that significant. But the affinities subsisting between Blake and Dylan extend far beyond merely superficial similarities. To begin on a level of high abstraction, which I aim to ground empirically in the course of this discussion: the poetry of Blake and Dylan shares a cluster of fundamental ideas, themes, feelings, images, and modes of expression. I am not here concerned with literary influences and borrowings—as Dylan has emphasized, "open up yer eyes an' yer ears an' yer influenced"[1]—but with radical affinities of attitude and outlook. The parallels between Blake and Dylan are so exciting because of the way in which their major concerns add up to identifiable themes and characteristic modes of perception, and these in turn generate similar frames of reference and related critical problems for the serious student of their work. And, in the case of Dylan, it should be noted that little commentary has risen much above the level of news-gossip. As Michael Gray has reminded us, while Dylan "the showbiz phenomenon" has been played up in A Big Way, "the real impact of Dylan's art has passed unnoticed by both the literati and the mass-media."[2]

The subjects that both Dylan and Blake address are chiefly of a religious and moral nature, although neither of them adheres to a traditional dogma. They are concerned in the largest terms—political, existential, metaphysical, psychological—with the perennial dilemmas of human existence that confront thinking man once he has left (to use Keats' phrase) the chamber of maiden thought. The group of related ideas and themes common to Blake and Dylan might be summed up as human freedom, dignity, integrity of experience, love and compassion as opposed to injustice,

---

[1] "My Life in a Stolen Moment," *Writings and Drawings by Bob Dylan* (New York: Alfred Knopf, 1973), p. 51. All quotations of Dylan's poems and songs up to 1971 will be from this text.
[2] *Song and Dance Man: The Art of Bob Dylan* (New York: E.P. Dutton, 1972), p. 6.

evil, inhumanity, hypocrisy, and indifference. Each poet is principally a humanist who employs his creative energies to affirm life when lived fully and in the flesh. Each, because he strives fiercely for the divine center of an unfallen humanity, at times violently rejects various forms of limitation imposed on man (by himself and by society) that violate or deny his true potential. For both, "life" is the irreducible mystery to be witnessed and celebrated. Blake chants repeatedly, "all that lives is holy," and Dylan, even when wounded and bleeding from the thorns of bitter Experience, is still able to embrace the very negations of his song in a larger affirmation, half-ironic, and half-filled with wonder: "But it's alright, Ma, it's life, and life only" ("It's Alright, Ma, I'm Only Bleeding"). Both confirm the value of *being* with a passionate, even reckless prodigality, and both condemn that which impedes the life flow. What Dylan said in an interview about "The Times They Are A-Changin'" is relevant to his larger vision: the battle hymn is not about the antagonism of youth and age as such; rather, at the time of writing the song, as he puts it, "those were the only words I could find to separate aliveness from deadness."[3] Blake's art is also concerned to sort out the quick from the moribund, from the compressed *Songs of Innocence and of Experience* (where youth and age also serve to symbolize modes of vision) to the expansive myth of the prophetic books. Both poets felt on their pulses that he who is not busy being born is busy dying.

"They're nothin! but the unwindin' of my happiness,"[4] wrote the early Dylan about his songs. The idea of the artist's work as the unfolding of his innermost self is also the clue to Romantic poetry, from Blake to D.H. Lawrence. The way in which the art of Blake and Dylan mirrors the unfolding of their happiness—and their unhappiness, one should add, for that is the shadow-side of Romantic joy—really comes down in the end to a question of salvation. For Dylan as well as for Blake, salvation is largely a matter of realizing the expression of a fuller humanity, individually and collectively. To them, it is not something we are born to, but something to be achieved—although the threshold of the higher humanity must always be rooted in the soil of our common biological male and femaleness. If for

---

[3]   Interview with Joseph Haas, *Chicago Daily News* (1965), rpt. in *Bob Dylan: A Retrospective*, ed. Craig McGregor (New York: William Morrow, 1972), pp. 110-111.

[4]   "Eleven Outlined Epitaphs," *Writings and Drawings*, p. 105.

Dylan and Blake we attain salvation through achieving the fullness of life, we are damned if our vitality is seriously impaired or denied. As Dylan sees it, "Lifelessness is the Great Enemy"[5] (and, as we discover in "Desolation Row," the great sin). Blake radically refashioned Christianity in his individualist mold to proclaim that only through the grace of freedom coupled with imagination can we reach the higher realms of genuine humanity: "I know of no other Christianity and of no other Gospel than the liberty of both body and mind to exercise the Divine Arts of Imagination" (*Jerusalem*). Lest we think otherwise, he explicitly states on several occasions that God is no more than the fulfillment of human potentialities through the exercise of imagination. In his humanology, God is no more than Man, and Man, at his best, is God. The context of Dylan's best songpoetry parallels Blake's idea that "all deities reside in the human breast" (*The Marriage of Heaven and Hell*), and the sentiment that he has Christ voice in a late poem, "Thou art a Man / God is no more / Thy own humanity learn to adore / For that is my Spirit of Life" ("The Everlasting Gospel"). When Crabb Robinson, puzzled by Blake's unorthodox Christianity, asked his opinion concerning "the imputed divinity of Christ," Blake replied with the kind of put-on that Dylan has perfected as an art: "He is the only God," but added, "And so am I, and so are you."[6] The quest for a more integral personhood that in Blake and Dylan becomes a concern with salvation and damnation remains for them chiefly a humanistic venture because they share the basic Romantic intuition that what we call "God" is only a cosmic, mythic projection of our profoundest self, or as Goethe put it in an aphorism, "Was der Mensch als Gott verehrt, / Ist sein eigenstes Innere herausgekehrt" ("What man reveres as God is his own inner being turned outward") .

---

[5]   Liner notes for *Highway 61 Revisited*, *Writings and Drawings*, p. 181.

[6]   *Reminiscences*, in *The Portable Blake*, ed. Alfred Kazin (New York: Viking, 1968), p. 680.

II

In an important essay, Steven Goldberg has pointed to Dylan as essentially a poet of salvation. But he pushes beyond this to claim, unequivocally, that "Bob Dylan is a mystic."[7] Now this is interesting because the history of Blake's literary fortunes shows that after he stopped being considered a madman at worst and a crank at best, he began to be increasingly described as a mystic. The consensus of the best modern Blake criticism, however, has rejected this tag. Northrop Frye, for one, emphasizes that Blake is a visionary, not a mystic, and his distinction is highly appropriate to Dylan's songpoetry:

> A visionary creates, or dwells in, a higher spiritual world in which the objects of perception in this one have become transfigured and charged with a new intensity of symbolism. This is quite consistent with art, because it never relinquishes the visualization which no artist can do without. It is a perceptive rather than a contemplative attitude of mind; but most of the greatest mystics, St. John of the Cross and Plotinus for example, find the symbolism of visionary experience not only unnecessary but a positive hindrance to the highest mystical contemplation. This suggests that mysticism and art are in the long run mutually exclusive, but that the visionary and the artist are allied.[8]

Mark Schorer too casts out the mystical for the visionary Blake:

> ... as the value of vision is the central fact in Blake's religion and aesthetics, so the sanctity of personality, individuality, is the central fact of his philosophy. The mystic silences the faculties and expels personality. Blake exalts personality and demands that it reintegrate its faculties.[9]

---

[7] Originally in *Saturday Review* (1970), rpt. in *Bob Dylan: A Retrospective*, p. 364.

[8] Northrop Frye, *Fearful Symmetry: A Study of William Blake* (Princeton: Princeton Univ. Press, 1947), p. 8.

[9] *William Blake: The Politics of Vision* (New York: Vintage, 1959), p. 6.

To adopt the terms of Frye's and Schorer's arguments, I maintain that the most fruitful literary approach to Dylan is to view him not as a mystic, but, in one leading aspect at least, as a Romantic visionary, or what Rimbaud called a *voyant*. What is more, the vision of Blake and Dylan is fundamentally a dual one. The hard-hitting protest of each against the life-denying forces which he perceives around him is in the first instance a passionate denunciation of the injustices perpetrated by an inhuman social order. But on a deeper level it is also an outcry against the confines of a fallen world of Experience, which must be reformed and renewed not primarily, or not only, through political action, but chiefly through individual vision and compassion. Only love can effect a genuine transformation of the inner self and the outer world, because the latter is chiefly an expression of the former. It is significant that in the development of both Blake and Dylan the theme of protest shifts increasingly from the social-political to the individual-metaphysical plane, a fact which also holds true for other Romantic visionaries, like Shelley.

The movement away from overt political radicalism to a more profoundly human espousal of love is evident in Blake's later prophetic books (especially *Jerusalem*, his crowning achievement) and in Dylan's albums beginning with *Bringing It All Back Home*. What John Beer has concluded about Blake's "cycle of ... development" holds true for Dylan's as well: "By the time that [Blake] wrote *Jerusalem* the vehemence of his early prophetic books had already disappeared. Indignation, protest, anger had given place to the belief that one force only could redeem mankind: the indwelling light of imaginative power which would release in men delight in creative power and a compassionate forgiveness."[10] In the later vision of Blake and Dylan the recovery of human integrity and wholeness and the return from alienation and lifelessness is the experience of love as a vast continuum of energy from the most intensely physical to the most refinedly spiritual, from the gorgeous genital "moment of desire" ("Visions of the Daughters of Albion") to the spirit that dwells in all of us as a joyfully felt presence. Both poets came to realize that the sufferings of man in the world of Experience are only a reflection of the failure of the Inner Man, Blake's

---

[10]   *Blake's Visionary Universe* (New York: Barnes & Noble, 1969), p. 296.

Imagination, to live up to his true potential. Once we begin to explore the possibilities of love and imagination, the sharp boundaries of experience will fade away, and man will stand newborn in all the naked radiance of his being, as he does in Blake's "Glad Day" painting.

It should also be pointed out that in the case of each artist, the version of their work that faces us on the printed page is only one dimension of a vision that is richer and fuller. For Blake and Dylan the script is not merely supplemented, respectively, by the addition of manuscript illumination and the presence of voice and melody; the overall effect depends as much on the prints and on the songs as it does on the poem-text. This means that, just as we have to make room for Blake's and Dylan's moral-religious concerns in a full evaluation of their art, we must also allow that one cannot really do justice to their achievement by sticking to strictly literary standards. This does not mean that such standards are to be held in abeyance, but rather, that they must be supplemented by other considerations if we are to be fair to either artist. If your aesthetics deny that religious concern can be fundamental to art, the way T.E. Hulme did when he dismissed Romanticism as "spilt religion," then you can't begin to come to terms with the overall impact of Blake's and Dylan's vision. And if you read Dylan without listening to the songs or the voice of the man who sings them, or if you declare, *ipso facto*, that they can't be poems because they are songs— and heaven help us, even hit ones at that—then you are simply limiting your own aesthetic appreciation, and not making a considered judgment.

III

If, as I have suggested, Blake and Dylan are both artists whose concerns are broadly religious and moral and whose vision is fundamentally a dual one, they also share a common ground in which it was nurtured—the prime source-book for vision, prophecy, wisdom and apocalypse in the West—the Bible. For Blake the Bible was the sacred code of art and the chief repository for the molds into which he cast the gigantic forms of his private mythology. As Beer has observed, he was inclined "to read the Bible basically as a visionary document" (*Blake's Visionary Universe*, p. 30). His work might be viewed as the crowning achievement of Protestant art in Britain. Dylan's art, too, is drenched in the Biblical context, and the vehement dissent of this Jewish son of the American middle class to the status quo might also be viewed—forgive the pun—in Protestant terms. Blake's way of reading the Bible, one suspects, is also Dylan's. To quote Beer again, from Blake's individualistic and independent approach to the sacred texts, "instead of a constant emphasis on the Law, there would emerge a series of accounts of prophets and seers protesting against the injustices of rulers looking to an ideal vision of man" (p. 33). Craig McGregor, among others, has noted the "use of Biblical symbol and allusion throughout "Dylan's work, and John Landau has written that the "righteous zeal" of a song like "Masters of War" is "vengeful in the Old Testament sense of the word."[11] In an 1968 interview, Dylan, when queried if he had read Kafka's *Parables and Paradoxes*, answered, "the only parables I know are the Biblical parables." On being asked, "when did you read the Bible parables," he replied, "I have always read the Bible, though not necessarily always the parables."[12]

The background of Biblical parable and prophecy helps to account, I think, for some of the parallels that one can find between the manner and method in the vision of Dylan and Blake. There is, for instance, an aphoristic brilliance and boldness in each that may have been fostered by a long acquaintance with the muscular speech rhythms of the King James Bible. Blake has been called "perhaps the finest gnomic artist in English literature,"[13] and a number of Dylan's more striking proverbs are in the process of passing from counterculture lingo into popular parlance: "don't follow leaders, watch parking meters," "when you got nothing, you

---

[11]   McGregor in the Introduction to *Bob Dylan: A Retrospective*, p. 12; Landau in a review of *John Wesley Harding* in *Crawdaddy* (1960) rpt. in *Retrospective*, p. 252.

[12]   "Conversations With Bob Dylan," by John Cohen and Happy Traum in *Sing Out!* (1968), rpt. in *Retrospective*, pp. 273-274.

[13]   Frye, *Fearful Symmetry*, p. 5.

got nothing to lose," "liberty is just equality in school," etc. There are even parallels in the ideas expressed in Blake's and Dylan's apothegms—for example, Blake's proverb of hell, "drive your cart and your plow over the bones of the dead," and Dylan's advice to Baby Blue to forget the dead she's left, because they will not follow her ("It's All Over Now, Baby Blue"). The imagery of both poets also owes a good deal to the Bible, particularly that of the apocalyptic, the grotesque, and the plainly weird. I suspect that the modes of symbolic apprehension involved in what Dylan has aptly described as his "chains of flashing imagery"[14] owe probably as much to the Old Testament as they do to the *symbolistes*. Perhaps here we also have an influence, and in this case an unfortunate one, on some of the more ponderous phrases the early Dylan perpetrated in the mode of the false sublime. The crimson flames which tie through his ears at the outset of "My Back Pages" smack of the high and mighty trap of post-adolescent Biblism.

IV

Like that of Blake, the development of Dylan from an involvement with political protest and the more topical issues of the day to an engagement with salvation and with the permanent politics of human nature can be clearly traced out in the succession of his major songpoetry. As I see it, his career as a Romantic is comprised of four stages to date: (1) protest on the verge of vision, (2) the flowering of vision, its frenzied disintegration and reconstitution on a higher level, (3) Dylan in Beulahland, and (4) the personal vision of love. These phases which I shall discuss in some detail do not constitute airtight compartments, nor should the boundaries between them be drawn too rigidly. As Blake said by way of humorous self-contradiction, "to generalize is to be an idiot." At best they might be viewed as a pocket map to Dylan's overall Romanticism. They delineate

---

[14] To Ralph Gleason ("The Children's Crusade," in *Ramparts*, 1966, rpt. in *Retrospective*, p. 173.)

13

the process of its ripening as well as the diverse aspects of this chameleon poet's variable identity. Further, they denominate states of mind through which Dylan has passed. As such, the problem of his identity vis à vis these phases is related to what Blake had to say about "states": "Man Passes on, but States remain for Ever; he passes thro' them like a traveller who may as well suppose the places he has passed thro' exist no more, as a Man may suppose that the States he has pass'd thro' Exist no more. Everything is Eternal" ("A Vision of the Last Judgement"). From this perspective, some of the states that Dylan has repudiated because he has moved on to some other place, are not irrelevant so long as they continue to speak to individuals undergoing that state.

1. Protest on the Verge of Vision

This is the early Dylan who made such powerful waves as the Pied Piper of a new generation challenging the strongholds of the Establishment with slogans, demonstrations, a keenly felt sense of moral superiority, and all the optimism of Innocence. It is the time when Dylan, as Joan Baez put it in a recent tribute, sang "those eloquent songs from the good old days / That set us to marching with banners ablaze" ("Winds of the Old Days"). Dylan's initial phase, which is represented by his first four albums (*Bob Dylan*, 1962; *The Freewheelin' Bob Dylan*, *The Times They Are A-Changin'*, 1963; *Another Side of Bob Dylan*, 1964), opens with the "Song to Woody," advances steadily to the verge of vision, of which we get some unadulterated glimpses, and closes irrevocably with Dylan's coming of age in "My Back Pages," his rite of passage to a new mode of sustained vision.

The only original material on Dylan's first release enforces his stance as the Romantic outsider who exists on the fringes of society and who, because he has no stake in it, can see it without blinders. Both songs point to Woody Guthrie as the formative influence on Dylan's poetic self-conception, one by way of imitation (talking blues), the other by way of homage. "Song to Woody" is imbued with the soulful wisdom of the wandering blues singers who blow in "with the dust and are gone with the wind." The folk troubadour is a man whose humanity is undiminished, and who has close ties to the earth and the elements. From this perspective he is aware of the fact that the world seems to be dying when it has not had a chance yet to be born. This is the visionary side Dylan will begin to play up in major key in later albums, along with the other side of his dual vision, the topical concern, which in "Talking New York" is touched upon as the fundamental lack of human decency in the modern city. As in the London of Blake's Experience, the atmosphere of Dylan's New York is wintry and cold; people are under the ground, and the only thing that reaches to the sky is concrete. The tone of Dylan's depiction of lifelessness is deftly humorous: people don't have enough to eat, but they do have the utensils with which to cut. The reader isn't savaged yet by his irony, but lightly introduced to his prevailing concern with resurrection and damnation. At the end of this saga of innocence, the pauper-son of the Western earth and inheritor of the elements turns from the freezing city and follows the life force, the sun, to—East Orange.

In the next three albums the topical and visionary concerns implicit in "Song to Woody" and "Talking New York" pick up amazing momentum, and the typical Dylan song of this period emerges as one that, whether comic-grotesque or serious-prophetic, packs a hell of a wallop. "The Excellence of every Art is its intensity," wrote John Keats, and Dylan now begins to overwhelm and stun us with that excellence. Especially when he fuses vision with moral outrage, he achieves a raw power that helps us overlook the fact that these songs are stewed in the juices of their own self-righteousness. In "Masters of War" Dylan presents his credentials as the outraged seer ("I can see through your masks") and purges his revulsion through the cleansing fires of sheer hatred. In songs like this where he draws a bead on the Enemy, he begins to sound distinctly like Blake. Frye's comment on the visionary protest of *The Songs of Experience* is also an apt description of "Masters of War": "contempt and horror have never spoken more clearly in English poetry" (*Fearful Symmetry*, p. 236). But the young folk-bard goes beyond Blake in his eagerness to hate to the hilt. Blake would not subscribe to the sentiment that even Jesus couldn't forgive

15

such crimes, nor would he gloat over the corpses of the war-makers being lowered into the ground.

The Blakean compression, vigor, and drive of phrase that mark "Masters of War" are supplemented by distinctly Blakean imagery in an early masterpiece like "A Hard Rain's A-Gonna Fall." Now the protest song is en route to genuine vision as the succession of flashing images piled one atop the other begins to symbolically focus the deeper ills of our fallen world with devastating impact—the new-born babe with wolves all around it, the black branch dripping blood, the rooms full of men with bleeding hammers, etc. Some of the images are more palpable hits than others, as Dylan searches to discover his distinctive vein of explosive metaphor and symbol, Blakean to the extent that they remind us of lines like "the hapless Soldier's sigh, / Runs in blood down Palace walls" ("London"). Much less successful because one-dimensional and yes—sentimental—are the ballads that focus on the stock victims and have-nots of society: Donald White, the petty criminal turned murderer because he was not allowed to remain in prison; Emmett Till the Negro lynched by the Klan; Davey Moore the boxer whose death implicates a whole society; and most stereotypical of all, the rich white master William Zanzinger who kills the poor black servant Hattie Carrol. Some of these protest and civil rights songs are far removed from vision because they are too much like ideological mock-ups of liberal white conscience. They do not succeed precisely because they do not spring from Dylan's own observation, whereas the ballads of the dispossessed and the done over that come from his own background have a force that propels the indictment of society to the level of vision. Songs like "Hollis Brown," "North Country Blues," and the superb "Percy's Song" redeem Dylan's balladry from the propagandistic marionette-theater effect because they are deeply rooted in Dylan's Midwestern childhood: "The town I grew up in is the one / That has left me with my legacy visions."[15]

"Percy's Song" is surely one of the very best efforts of the early Dylan. This spontaneous overflow of powerful feelings at the news of the ninety-nine year prison sentence of a friend for manslaughter (because of a car

---

[15] "Eleven Outlined Epitaphs," *Writings and Drawings*, p. 101.

accident) conveys a very Blakean sense of the Law with the image of the judge's frozen face, as he speaks out of the corner of his mouth in explaining the impossible verdict to his bewildered questioner. The song clearly demonstrates Dylan's dual outlook, because the friend's misfortune is partly the fault of a simple twist of fate, and partly that of a grotesquely inhuman application of the letter of the law. Dylan's tragic realization that "what happened to him / Could have happened to anyone" is that of Innocence trying to come to terms with the thorns of Experience.

The sensational impact of Dylan's first phase is in part due to what Landau has described as "the myth of the adolescent, the myth of self-righteousness, the myth of our own purity."[16] In some of the more shallow songs the guileless *me* versus the guilty *them* is rather blatant. These pieces imply— and got—strong audience identification. The issue is really we goodies shouting down those baddies, with God on our side: Dylan could turn his trenchant irony on the self-righteousness of others, but his own purity was still above reproach. The poet of *John Wesley Harding* who identifies with the guilt of those who put Saint Augustine out to death, and who writes, "in the day of confession, we cannot mock a soul" ("Too Much of Nothing") is still a long way down the road of hard-won maturity. The myth of one's own rightness is also strong in some of Dylan's early love songs, like "Don't Think Twice" and "It Ain't Me, Babe," where he comes down pretty hard on what Blake attacked as the Female Will—women who not only want your heart, but your soul; who script you as their dream lover, and then some. To wit, Blake's proverb, "he who binds to himself a joy, / Does the winged life destroy" ("Eternity"). And so Dylan heads on down the road.

The fantastic, satirical humor of a number of his early compositions ("Talkin' World War III Blues," "Talkin' John Birch Paranoid Blues," "Motorpsycho Nightmare") is an indication that self-righteousness might one day be subject to its own deflation, and there are other signs as well to suggest that he is ready to move on, and that his growth, like that of most major artists, will be self-corrective. The forced rhetoric of his protest songs

---

[16]   *Retrospective*, p. 251.

sounds a false note next to the Wordsworthian eloquence of the elements, and so he wants to lay down his weary tune. He seems also to have tired rapidly of the savior and spokesman of the younger generation role, even though as late as the apocalyptic "Chimes of Freedom" he is still willing to carry the burden of the multitude of the "confused, accused, misused, strung-out" and to feel, somewhat ambitiously, a responsibility toward "every hung-up person in the whole wide universe." Yet there is also a new note of maturity in his delicate pity for the solitary grief of lovers and the pain of the harmless, tender souls shoved in prison.

The new tenderness is present as well in one of his loveliest songs, "To Ramona," which I find utterly astonishing in its ferocious poignancy. As a symbol of threatened, fragile life in a brute, insensate, death bound world, this lyric is light years more sophisticated than the moral hyping and typing of "Emmett Till." The dismissal of the death forces through a kind of aristocratic disregard—"there's no use in tryin' / T'deal with the dyin'"— is much more effective than the self-righteous battle-charge of the earlier incantations against evil. Dylan's sorrow for the sufferings of Ramona trapped in the rigid lines and fixed networks of Experience more than compensates for some of his earlier lapses. It shows his growing realization that whatever "freedom" is, it is not, beyond a very obvious level, a matter of legislative politics, but of the politics of experience. As Dylan had already told Nat Henthoff in 1964, "I looked around and saw all these people pointing fingers at the bomb. But the bomb is getting boring, because what's wrong goes much deeper than the bomb. What's wrong is how few people are free."[17]

Such an insight signals the end of Dylan's first stage. The year before, in "Bob Dylan's Dream," he had already envisioned a painful separation from a past where it was as easy to tell black from white as it was to sort out wrong from right. Now a year later in "My Back Pages," he says farewell to the arms of political protest, and prepares himself for another kind of song. He has learned a thing or two about the heated pride of aggressive

---

[17]   "The Crackin', Shakin', Breakin' Sounds," in *The New Yorker* (1964), rpt. in *Retrospective*, p. 56.

18

idealism, the idiocy of equating liberty with equality, and the terrible fact that in single mindedly dedicating oneself against something, we become progressively more like it. With a courageous prodigality, he dismisses his visions so far as those of a corpse evangelist, even as the art of a truer self beckons to him.

2. The Flowering of Vision, Its Collapse and Reintegration

The album sequence extending from *Bringing It All Back Home* (1965) to *John Wesley Harding* (1968) chronicles Dylan's emergence as a full-fledged visionary, the acceleration of that vision to the point of frenzy and its subsequent disintegration because of his having grabbed for too much, too fast; and finally, its triumphant re-emergence on a higher spiritual plane after he had picked up the pieces that went down in the flood.

Because of its comparatively greater variety and complexity, the song·poetry of the second phase does not lend itself as easily to categorization or summary. It moves between the poles of romantic idyll and grotesque nightmare, of magical realism and realized fantasy, of savage denunciation and joyous hymn. In *Bringing It All Back Home* the denunciation is there in "Maggie's Farm" and "It's Alright, Ma," the idyll in "Love Minus Zero / No Limit," the fantasy in "Mr. Tambourine Man," the hymn in "Gates of Eden," and the nightmare in "It's All Over Now, Baby Blue." The clearly major "Mr. Tambourine Man" reveals Dylan becoming more conscious of his gifts as a visionary, for it is an ode to his imagination. To reductively label it a drug-song says a good deal about the mindscape of 1960's hip culture. From this point of view, presumably Blake's *Jerusalem* would be no more than the day-trip of a Timothy Leary, and his Los, the Man with the Golden Arm. The appeal to the imagination in "Mr. Tambourine Man" to liberate the sense-stripped, deadened existence of modern nowhereman, and lead him to dance with the elements "far from the twisted reach of crazy sorrow" is also heard in "It's Alright, Ma," where Dylan's imagery pounds against the strait jackets fashioned for us by "society's pliers." Both poems reflect Blake's visionary imagination and concentrated power of phrasing. The "mind-forged manacles" that Dylan attacks in the latter make up a catalogue of some of the attributes of Blake's Experience—lifelessness, despair, repressive authority, senile complacency. Its companion piece, "Gates of Eden," can only point, by negative implication, to what the condition of an unfallen humanity might be: everything there is simply the opposite of what prevails in the kingdoms of Experience. The only positives that Dylan can identify with Eden form the holy trinity of the concluding stanza: love, dawn, and dream. But for the nonce these are silent miracles which elude the nets of language. "Gates of Eden" invites comparison with Blake's *Songs of Innocence and of Experience*, and Michael Gray has gone so far as to claim that "it is the major Dylan song that is most like Blake, and like the most characteristic Blake at that" (*Song and Dance Man*, p. 81).

The insanity and the *rigor mortis* that define life on Maggie's Farm become the visionary center of Dylan's next album, *Highway 61 Revisited* (1965). Dylan went rock and electric here, and the overall effect is that of a roller coaster ride through a contemporary Inferno. Now Dylan also approaches a level of symbolism that is analogous to Blake's use of personal myth in the prophetic books, for some of the elements of Dylan's unsystematic symbology recreate in their own terms some of the categories of Blake's. The great enemy Lifelessness, a corrosive spirit emanating from what Dylan in the *Playboy* interview humorously called the "anti-happiness committee" ("men and women who look like cigars") is the Urizen of Dylan's mid-sixties freak-show. Desolation Row, the underside of America the Beautiful, is doubtless the *pièce de resistance* of his grotesque, apocalyptic mode.

In a magic theater of the surreal and the absurd, Dylan projects a Blakean vision of the contemporary American metropolis. For me it is the most successful and sustained longpoem of his middle period because it does not dissolve in a labyrinth of private associations. Its uncanny collage of the most realistic with the most bizarre makes it simultaneously a personal vision and, as Gray has described it, "a brilliant political analysis of American society" (*Song and Dance Man*, p. 176) that probes far deeper than the earlier protest songs. The incredible imagery plants depth charges that explode our ordinary frames of reference and force us willy-nilly, by a method of disorientation, into a visionary state. Although the logic of the poem may escape us, the imagery and mood are carefully controlled for maximum effect: Dylan loads every rift with ore. From the ominous "they" at the outset, the imagery of disaster and of stunted, violated, unreal life begins to accumulate spectacularly: hanging, drowning (Ophelia, the Titanic), blindness (the commissioner), repressed or perverted sexuality, the complements of riot squad and ambulance, Dr. Filth's nurse and the cyanide hole, the heart attack machine, etc. The zany images and bizarre allusions ricochet off each other, tracing further patterns of meaning: for Ophelia who has gone down in the flood, Noah's rainbow can hold out no promise; her iron vest is a symbolic chastity belt that suffocates her vitality. The references to burning—insurance men with kerosene, Nero (who burned Rome)—conjure the violence implicit in the frustration of eros. And the Titanic, arrogant symbol of hope and progress, sailing at dawn is a diabolic touch: images of ultimate disaster and archetypal hope are ironically juggled. The network of allusion in the poem indicates that Dylan may have gone to school to Eliot's *Waste Land* for his own visionary purposes. But his surreal treatment of the wasteland theme is ultimately still more hopeful than Eliot's *recherché* pessimism, because the elemental imagery toward the end (mermaids, fishermen, etc.), even if an echo of Prufrock, affirms life in spite of all that man can do to blight it. Eliot's disillusionment is resigned; Dylan's is charged with rebellion.

Most sinister of all is the darkness that threatens to engulf Desolation Row. The sun doesn't shine on it, and even the moon and the stars are fading out. The curtains which have been nailed across the street further reinforce this pattern of darkness and entombment. Indeed, a larger vision of death and suffocation prevails throughout *Highway 61 Revisited* fairly consistently— life-in-death in the "fact'ry" in "Tombstone Blues"; Rue Morgue Avenue and Melinda, the goddess of gloom; and an Eastertime where nobody can be resurrected, in "Just Like Tom Thumb's Blues"; and the "he" who "sits in your room, his tomb" in "Can You Please Crawl Out Your Window?" (a song not finally included on the record).

"Like a Rolling Stone," the high voltage jolter which opens *Highway 61 Revisited*, is the key to the state of mind which produced it and the subsequent double-disc, *Blonde on Blonde* (1966). The visionary who chronicles the desolation of urban civilization is a desperado voyant who achieves his novel perspective only because he has brutally cut himself off from a collective identity, so that he is completely on his own, with "no direction home." But the rolling stone metaphor implies that the disoriented seer, as he gathers momentum, will experience a crash landing. The most famous Dylan song of all is at least as much a self-confrontation as it is an attack on anybody else: Dylan realizes where he's come from to achieve his radical singleness of being, and he also anticipates the inevitable fall he must experience if he goes further to the brink of vision. As is evident from interviews around this time, he was moving at an unprecedented speed, and what is more, was probably fairly heavily into the drug scene as well. The frenetic mood and frenzied imagery of *Blonde on Blonde* produce new creative highs and powerfully weird effects before lapsing into incoherence and self-indulgence. Some of the most striking phrases, images, and musical moments that Dylan ever produced are to be found in "Visions of Johanna"—"ghost of 'lectricity howls in the bones of her face" is seared with acid strength in our consciousness before Dylan loses his vision in the rain, and begins to babble like one of the neon madmen. "Sad-Eyed Lady of the Lowlands" may represent an ultimate effort to salvage the vision. With its "mercury mouth" and "sheet-metal memory of Cannery Row" it is one of the most haunting and exotic things he has ever done. The "saint like face" that lights up the last stanza of this hypnotic songpoem strengthens my intuition that, like many of his mysterious female figures, the sad-eyed lady is a personification of Dylan's anima[18] mourning from deep within the disintegration of his personality.

18   In Jungian psychology, "the anima is a personification of all feminine psychological tendencies in a man's psyche, such as vague feelings and moods, prophetic hunches, receptiveness to the irrational, capacity for personal love, feelings for nature, and ... his relations to the unconscious." Especially for the

After *Blonde on Blonde* came the legendary motorcycle accident (July 1966), followed by Dylan's retreat from being a public personality and performing artist. *The Basement Tape*, the record of Dylan's private jam session with the Band while he was recuperating in seclusion (finally released in 1974 after a number of bootlegs), reveals his spiritual consolidation and visionary reintegration that accounts for the profoundly changed poet of *John Wesley Harding*. In many of the cuts he does with the Band he is attempting to come to terms with the crack-up of his speeding vision, and his near brush with death, which for him was probably only the logical culmination of the direction implicit in his life and work since "Like a Rolling Stone." After the debacle he seems eager to reconnect his roots to the soil of ordinary humanity. For the next few years his marriage and family life become increasingly important for sustaining his identity, and creative partnership with congenial professionals is a further means of getting back in touch, as the relaxed mood of *The Basement Tape* indicates. "Down in the Flood" is a retrospective meditation on the disaster for which he had headed, and "This Wheel's on Fire" seems to be a coming to terms with the psychic significance of the motorcycle crash. "Tears of Rage," "Too Much of Nothing," and "Nothing Was Delivered" similarly seem to turn a critical eye on his own achievement so far, although the lyrics are fragmentary and none too clear. And the delightfully ribald overtones of a number of songs also suggest the resurgence of ordinary human interests in his poetry.

With *John Wesley Harding* (1968) Dylan re-emerges publicly with an altered but restored and even more potent vision than hitherto. This collection of tightly-knit songs may well be the best work he has produced to date. The nightmare painting of *Blonde on Blonde* gives way to a lean and quiet contemplative strength that attests a mastery of his materials that had been progressively lost in the mad acceleration of his imagination. The album is deeply religious and moral; it is, in the words of Anthony Scaduto, "Dylan's version of the Bible, songs written as parables describing the fall

---

artist the function of "the anima as a guide to the inner world" is of paramount importance. *Man and His Symbols*, ed. Carl G. Jung (New York: Doubleday, 1964), pp. 177, 186.

and rebirth of one man—Bob Dylan."[19] *John Wesley Harding* parallels the movement of the later Blake to "an increasing preoccupation with the 'mental' patterns that underlie the flux of human events" (*Blake's Visionary Universe,* pp.76-77). As such, it is not only a soul-searching self-portrait and confession of Bob Dylan, but also a visionary probing of the abiding spiritual realities of salvation and damnation. Because the album takes a number of Dylan's major themes to a higher level, it shows the artist's path as a spiral one which rounds back upon itself with progressively increasing subtlety of awareness. The song for which the album is named again depicts the Romantic outsider, now an American Robin Hood and folk hero who robs the rich but who never hurt an honest man, and who lives the myth of freedom: nobody can "track or chain him down."

Subsequent songs deal on a level ranging from Biblical myth to American folk-legend with related figures—the loving, the lost, the unfree, the guilty, and the damned—which are probably in part symbolic projections of Dylan's psyche. As Dylan told Scaduto, "I discovered that when I used words like 'he' and 'it' and 'they' and talking about other people, I was really talking about nobody but me. I went into *John Wesley Harding* with that knowledge in my head" (*Bob Dylan,* p. 249). These representative figures, in other words, dramatize aspects of the Self as it is to be seen daily in all of us—thus the new universality of Dylan's more personal art. It is no longer *us* versus *them,* it is now we who are confronted with ourselves as Dylan turns the mirror of his art on his inner being. The rhetoric of condemnation has been replaced with compassion and pity.

A number of the songs belong to the genre of the Romantic visionary lyric that Karl Kroeber has defined as "a poem which celebrates the experience, the insight, or simply the pattern of images occurring to the poet in a trance, when dreaming, or under the influence of a preternatural vision."[20] In "As I Went Out One Morning" the speaker is looking for Tom Paine, legendary hero of the American dream of freedom. Instead he finds "the

---

[19]   *Bob Dylan: An Intimate Biography* (New York: Grosset & Dunlap, 1971) p. 249.

[20]   *Romantic Narrative Art* (Madison: Univ. of Wisconsin Press, 1966), p.51.

fairest damsel / That ever did walk in chains," who wants to seduce him into an alliance with her. Whatever else she may stand for, betrayal of freedom and integrity is clearly a part of her plan. The speaker is saved in the nick of time by the appearance of Tom Paine himself, who apologizes for her behavior. In this poem the persona has been able to maintain his integrity, but in another searching dream vision, "I Dreamed I Saw St. Augustine," he is among those who put the Biblical prophet of resurrection ("Arise, arise, he cried so loud") out to death. The realization in the dream of his complicity and guilt is conveyed with shattering poignancy that is something genuinely new in Dylan's poetry. He wakes up alone, terrified; he bows his head and cries.

The latter-day parable of Frankie Lee the gambler and Judas Priest further chronicles the loss of integrity and the fact of damnation as Frankie Lee mistakes the blandishments of Judas Priest—money and slavish sensual indulgence—for eternity and paradise. Fittingly enough, he dies of thirst in the arms of his betrayer after a seventeen day romp in his temple of earthly delights. If for Blake, the priests, enforcers of institutionalized religion, bind with briars his joys and desires ("The Garden of Love") and demonstrate that soul without eros is a charnel house, for Dylan the parable of Lee and Priest shows that pleasure without soul is equally lethal. Other songs focus the threats to integrity of self and spirit with equal force. "Dear Landlord" is partly a plea for a valuation of the individual in non-commercial, non-materialistic terms: "please don't put a price on my soul." "I Am a Lonesome Hobo" is the cautionary confession of a man who lived by the Urizenic virtues of deceit, blackmail, mistrust and jealousy. He prospered in judging others, but in the process lost his soul. In passing judgment on himself at the end of the song, there is hope, paradoxically, that he is on the road to regaining it. The Wicked Messenger (the mockingbird in Dylan) is a near cousin of his who also is on the path to redemption with the insight that "If ye cannot bring good news, then don't bring any."

"I Pity the Poor Immigrant" may be the finest song on the album in the visionary mode. The poor immigrant is representative of a state of mind which thrives on denying life and joy in all its facets. Not wishing to be

25

alive himself, he tries to put out the spark in others. The result of all his evil striving is impotent frustration and aloneness. Between hating life and fearing death, he has absolutely nothing to call his own. Dylan offers him something precious: a vision of utter compassion and forgiveness. *John Wesley Harding* ends, appropriately enough, with two love songs, as the theme of compassion is at once broadened and intensified into passion itself. Unlike the poor immigrant whose visions must shatter like glass once consummated, Dylan's visions culminate in the achievement of gladness and joy, even if their celebration at the conclusion of his great middle period is couched in earthy clichés, "I'll be your baby tonight."

3. Bob Dylan in Beulahland

In Blake's myth, Beulah is partly the earthly paradise of sexual love. He took the name from *Isaiah* (where it refers to Palestine, the married land). Presided over by the moon, this region of sensual fulfilment provides a welcome "refuge from the gigantic warfare of ideas in Eternity; here flock all those who are exhausted, the weak … to rest in sleep."[21] For those who remain too long in Beulah's pastoral landscape of hills, rivers, valleys, and vegetation, it is also a place to vegetate.

Bob Dylan settles rather happily into Beulahland in his third phase, which extends from *Nashville Skyline* (1969) to *New Morning* (1970). He explores its geography and hymns the milk and honey pleasures of its earth. By the time of *New Morning* he has settled in so snugly that vision gives way frequently to down-home platitudes, sung with the best will in the world. Although his feelings seem as fresh as ever, the forms in which he couches them are pretty much old hat. The quiet enjoyments of Beulahland are not conducive to energetic exertions in the way of original perception or

---

[21]   S. Foster Damon, *A Blake Dictionary: The Ideas and Symbols of William Blake* (Providence: Brown Univ. Press, 1965), p. 43. For a concise summary of the role of Beulah in Blake's four-fold vision see also John Beer, *Blake's Humanism* (New York: Barnes & Noble, 1968), p. 33.

expression—time sure passes slowly when you're lost in Beulah's dream, watching the river flow. Instead of poetry, the languid joys of Beulah give rise to Paul McCartney fluff like "in harmony with the cosmic sea / … love needs no company" ("If Dogs Run Free"), or issue in the moonglow bathos of "Winterlude, this dude thinks you're fine."

While they clearly usher in stage three, the folksy clichés that conclude *John Wesley Harding* act as a glossy varnish for the deeper, visionary and moral concerns of the album, and the authentic welling up of gladness that they express ("my little bundle of joy") keeps the truth from becoming a mere truism. In *Nashville Skyline*, however, truth begins its slide into conventionality, even though Dylan still succeeds here and there in rendering the moment of desire with a funky immediacy of feeling and a freshness of language ("Lay, lady, lay, lay across my big brass bed") and in finding original phrases ("rivers that ran through ev'ry day"). In *New Morning*, ironically, more of the freshness is lost to platitudes in what Gray calls an "exquisite, ethereal pastoral conceit" (*Song and Dance Man*, p. 291) which becomes, for my taste, too much of a sleepy idyll. Individual vision gives way to sentimental stereotyping. In "Sign on the Window" the speaker wants to have a place in Utah, a wife, and a pile of kids who call him Dad: "that must be what it's all about." Aw, shucks. In "Father of Night" original perception is forfeited for a traditional hymn (and admittedly, a moving one) to the "Commander-in-Chief" of "Tombstone Blues," or Blake's "old Nobodaddy," and in the touching "If Not For You" salvation becomes too much like marriage. As for the songs which are not country, a little vision is cut with a lot of bathos—"Day of the Locusts," "Went to See the Gypsy," and "Three Angels" might be Songs of Experience updated and rewritten as muzak.

Actually, the third phase says nothing but good things about Dylan's larger humanity. It was a kind of salvation for him to put down roots and to warble the most ordinary tunes of daily life. But the pastoral/domestic experience, while vital for his personal growth and happiness, is a pretty thin vein for his art. He would have to move on before it collapsed into mere mannerism, and he did: not by repudiating it, but by injecting vision back into the golden legend, and by bringing a tense realism and an energetic selfhood to the hazy romance of love.

4. The Personal Vision of Love

With the release of the single "George Jackson" in 1971, Dylan's vision comes roaring back. In his outraged grief, he makes the shooting of Jackson symbolic of the destruction of the spirit of love and freedom by the vindictive powers who rule the kingdoms of experience. The authorities who locked Jackson away for a seventy dollar robbery are themselves the prisoners of their visionless negation of compassion. Unreal themselves, "frightened of his power … scared of his love," they cut him down "because he was just too real." The only power they possess is that to destroy. Unlike the bewildered speaker of the earlier "Percy's Song," that of "George Jackson" knows, on a visionary level, the why and wherefore of what happened. His dual vision fuses the political and the spiritual with a focused clarity that rises above the temptation to hate. The authorities are as much the victims of their blindness as Jackson is of his realness. The Blakean bard who sings the ballad of both recognizes that the potential of Jackson's love-power, like the fear-hatred of the authorities, is present in all of us, which makes the song ultimately as much a matter of hope as of despair and grief.

If "George Jackson" takes its subject of destroyed freedom from current American events, the "Billy" ballad (1973) of Dylan's sound track for Peckinpah's film, *Pat Garrett and Billy the Kid*, refracts the same theme through the romantic legend of the Western outlaw. The film assignment was as if made to order for Dylan, who had celebrated the Romantic outsider-rebel from Jessie James to Woody Guthrie and John Wesley Harding. By the time Dylan finished with the song, he transformed the folk-tale of Billy the Kid into a tragic Western mythos, a vision of the betrayal and destruction of the innocent American dream of freedom and integrity. Ironically, the Judas who sells Billy out is his friend Pat Garrett, bought over by the corrupt businessmen who cannot afford the challenge of Billy's free and noble spirit. Like George Jackson, he is too much of a threat because he is too real, too self-perfected. An American Christ-figure, he is tracked and chained down—unlike John Wesley Harding—by the unfree who want to make inroads on his manly spirit and his soul. The issue of freedom is again related to that of love: Dylan makes clear that Billy was a loving man, who knew how to "spend a night with some sweet senorita," and whose passing will be hymned by a tragic chorus of gypsy queens. In some ways the "Billy" ballad is Dylan's most representative song to date because it seems to touch in one way or another on most of his major themes. The incredible voice that sings it in three different versions is suffused with a timeless sorrow and gritty pathos, which communicates tremendously the vision inherent in his handling of the Billy the Kid legend.

The emotional energy recaptured in these songs carries over into Dylan's most recent albums, *Planet Waves* (1974), *Blood on the Tracks* (1974) and *Desire* (1975), where the vision of love as salvation, grown insipidly one-dimensional in the country idyll of the third phase, is revitalized and authenticated in a lean and vigorous new confessional poetry. In *Planet Waves* he celebrates what Blake called the lineaments of gratified desire with an eroticism that runs the gamut from fiery passion to tender intimacy. From the Lawrentian perspective of phallic marriage Dylan reviews the past and realizes how much he has been living on the road, and how close he has come to the edge of the abyss: "I was in a whirlwind, now I'm in a better place" ("Something There Is About You"). Lines of original metaphor and brilliant phrasing are interlaced with clichés and ordinary slang that make for a poetic realism which documents complex shades of passion. And strong tensions and countercurrents of feeling are introduced that make some of the lines crackle with energy: "I hate myself for loving you" ("Dirge"). The two best songpoems are the concluding hymns on each side, "Forever Young" and "Wedding Song." The former, really as much a prayer for himself as for his children, is a Romantic ode to joy which commemorates the season of youth not as a matter of age, but as a state of mind. It is an eloquent address to his source of vision as an artist, and a talisman for its persistence in the future. The latter is Dylan's most mature love lyric. Instead of looking back to the high points of the past, it anticipates in a dynamic sense the passionate moments and rich continuity of the future. In Biblical speech rhythms, he firmly repudiates the savior, warrior-of-truth stance of the past, and affirms the elemental primacy of human passion in terms of a personal commitment to love at which he himself cannot cease to marvel. His wife turns the tide on him each day, and teaches his eyes to see. Love is the basis of all higher vision.

In "Wedding Song," Dylan's passion anticipates the future rather than living off the past: he will love her more than ever, "now that the past is gone." In *Blood on the Tracks*, conversely, he turns to a visionary exploration of the meaning of the past through songs that recapitulate various love relationships. While the confessional vein remains strong as he speaks through the mouths of different personae, it is now integrated within a fictional frame. Many of the songs "replay the past" ("If You See Her Say Hello") to ferret out the fundamental meaning of the politics of passion. As Dylan explores the fate of romantic love in the realms of Experience, he achieves an insight both personal and universal in probing the eternal verities implicit in the crossing of individual lives. There is also a new mastery in his handling of language, and in his assured shifts from incandescent images to gnomic and proverbial phrases.

"Simple Twist of Fate" captures the irrational force of love which can whirl us about and leave us stranded in a more quiet but empty place longing for the past. The sensuous, erotic spark that ignites passion is evoked in the poem through a series of brilliant metaphors. "Idiot Wind" is the most challenging vision of the past on the album. It invites comparison with "Like a Rolling Stone" because of its heartfelt mood of denunciation. But now the attack is explicitly directed against the self as well as the other, as Dylan is no longer able to dissociate himself from the blame: "it's a wonder *we* can even feed ourselves." The cryptic tone of this visionary ode is reminiscent of *Highway 61 Revisited*, as are some of the grotesque and surreal motifs, and the charged, flashing imagery is reminiscent of an even earlier Dylan. The ferocious indictment seems to work on at least three levels: the "you" of the song is a woman, but also Dylan himself, and the

Idiot Wind generally, which is a sort of visionary objective correlative for the utter inanities that blow through the world of Experience, wrecking human joy and peace of mind. The Idiot Wind, the grotesque converse of visionary inspiration, is the distortion of truth through rumor, the abuse of language as trivial gossip, the self-preening display of learning, the petty malice and jealousy that can render our lives so null.

Some of the other songpoems on the album recoup previous Dylan modes or extend their relevance in new contexts. "Rosemary and the Jack of Hearts" is an absurdist parable in the vein of the ballad of Frankie Lee and Judas Priest which successfully pits the Jack of Hearts against Big Jim, a Western godfather type. The lovely "If You See Her, Say Hello" explores the tension between the claims of love and freedom. At the end of the song the speaker respects the lover who left him for "getting free," although he can't quite get free from "the bitter taste" of her departure, which "still lingers on." "Shelter From the Storm" is a confessional piece which focuses the danger of identifying salvation with a female madonna, and of projecting into that religious image the locus of one's identity and meaning in life. It may be rough out there in the storm, but the female shelter may turn out to be a prison. From this vantage point the comfy love and country nirvana of *New Morning* takes on quite a different coloring—the poet had bargained for salvation, and got "a lethal dose." The astringent vigor of phrasing is highly effective here, as is the vivid colloquialism of "Buckets of Rain," which with its simple gnomic verses affirms that love, despite its miseries, redeems life from bleakness: Dylan has become a stoic Romantic—"Life is sad, / Life is a bust"—but love is still its focal point.

Planet Waves and *Blood on the Tracks* reflect the personal love vision of a mature poet who, assured of his craft and confident of his powers, renders it from the piercing longing of eros aroused, to the Lawrentian struggles and ambivalences inherent in any passionate relationship, to the more mysterious current of affection which binds the world together into a living whole. These things, he implies, are there for us to see and experience, if we aren't blinded by the Idiot Wind. Dylan's most recent album, *Desire*, may be considered a further consolidation of the prophetic

31

and erotic elements of his art into a bardic songpoetry of elemental passion. In performing the songs on stage with the full complement of The Rolling Thunder Revue, Dylan presented himself in whiteface as a sort of Biblical shaman, performing a tribal ritual of plain speaking, soothsaying, healing, and confession. He rolls his thunder self-righteously with the heavy protest-rhetoric of "Hurricane" Carter, the black fighter as outlaw and victim of society, framed and locked away by the "pig-circus" of an evil judicial system. But there is also an intensely lyrical side to the album, especially in the song to his wife, where Dylan poignantly confesses his "unworthiness." A new, humbled Dylan emerges here, one strong enough to bare his human weaknesses, without games.

If "Sara" carries the burden of naked confession and desire, several other songs turn to myth and symbol to project human passion in its eternal forms. Dylan's affective identity is not only bound up in Sara, the mystical wife, but also in "Oh, Sister," his Biblical double and twin, and in the mysterious mother-sister-child figure of the ambitious symbolist longpoem, "Isis." Dylan's version of the Egyptian myth seems to be veiled confession, parable, and visionary narrative, all wrapped up in one. Its drama turns on temptation, death, and rebirth, with Dylan as the Osiris who is destroyed and reborn through Isis. The song's version of the eternal feminine seems again to invite a Jungian perspective in its use of the Isis myth for the rendering of positive and negative anima images.

The fact that a number of songs on *Desire* are conceived and executed on a somewhat lesser level of poetic and musical mastery may only indicate the impromptu nature of Dylan's performance both on the record and the Rolling Thunder tour: the currents of "desire" can be intense, but also spontaneous, even casual. The long "Joey" ballad, for instance, is mostly sentimental—the Mafia mobster as sweet old man and victim—and "Mozambique" is a set color-and-atmosphere piece that Frank Sinatra could comfortably sing in a Las Vegas lounge. "Romance in Durango" too is picturesque atmosphere painting ("hot chili peppers in the blistering sun"), but the romantic scenario of the two young lovers on the run has, in outline form, all the raw power of a Peckinpah film. And "Black Diamond

32

Bay," which carries on in the surreal tradition of "Rosemary and the Jack of Hearts," is also quite cinematic, and might have been written by Joseph Conrad on LSD. Like Blake, Dylan is able to have vision and humor coexist side-by-side, without one undercutting the other. In sum, Dylan's latest work is still very much in the Romantic line of vision. As Allen Ginsberg, the latter-day American beat-Blake and Rolling Thunder guru, assures us on the liner-notes to the album, the voice of *Desire* is that of "ancient blood singing," of "another great surge of unafraid prophetic feeling."

V

From this detailed mapping of the development of Dylan's vision through four stages it should be apparent that it does not, like Blake's, generate a system of myth. Blake's cosmic factoring of human faculties results in a larger mythology of the fall and reintegration of Universal Man whose vocabulary and universe of relations, have to be learned in order to be fathomed. Dylan's vision is not thus imaginatively autonomous, but much more immediately rooted, even at its most nightmarish fringes, in the ordinary facts of human experience, as is his idiom, which always derives from the living tradition of common Anglo-American speech patterns, ranging from the Bible translations to American street *patois* and hip talk. In this regard, Dylan's poetry might be seen as the missing link between the two greatest English Romantics, Blake and Wordsworth, between the poet of *The Marriage of Heaven and Hell* and that of the *Lyrical Ballads*. Dylan's art, like Blake's, does achieve the stature of vision, but it only approaches myth in a few songs like "Desolation Row" and "Visions of Johanna." For the most part it shies away from autonomous myth-making to return to the Wordsworthian sublime which produces its extraordinary effects from the most commonplace events of daily life, something which, as a matter of fact, is not alien to the more forthright Blake, who knows that to see imaginatively is "To see a World in a Grain of Sand / And a Heaven in a

Wild Flower / Hold Infinity in the palm of your hand / And Eternity in an hour" ("Auguries of Innocence").

The obvious question with which to end is, "what's next for Dylan?" My guess would be, an assimilation of his previous phases, plus a further refinement and development of his major themes from *Bob Dylan* to *Blood on the Tracks* and *Desire*. The many changes and reincarnations he has already gone through in his amazing career as a singer-poet-visionary bring to mind the examples of Keats and Rimbaud, except that Dylan has managed to survive, unlike them, to nearly middle age. Despite his famous frailty, he has exhibited an incredible staying power. So far, by not letting himself get caught in a groove, he has successfully lived the romantic credo of becoming over being, and proven the sincerity of his interview comment in 1966 that "decay turns me off. I'll die before I decay."[22]

Dylan has successfully eluded the demands of his audience when these conflicted with his remaining true to his art. Gravity hasn't pulled him down: he has always flown far above most of his fans, from the days when he traded in his acoustic guitar for a rock group and freaked out the folkniks, to the time when he went into retirement to come to terms with himself after the motorcycle accident. The aura of celebrity can be as much of a trap as the penumbra of obscurity. William Blake didn't let the latter keep him from being true to his art; in spite of all indignities, neglect, and privations, he refused to sell out to the tastes of his contemporaries and to the fads of the day. After a period of initial dismay and frustration at his failure to achieve even minimal success as a commercial artist, he cheerfully followed the light of his inner vision wherever it led. He kept the faith: "I laugh & sing, for if on Earth neglected I am in heaven a Prince among Princes, & even on Earth beloved by the Good as a Good Man." His guiding star, like that of all great artist-visionaries, was what he called "my own Self Will." Dylan too has so far demonstrated an ample talent for self-will or what Hermann Hesse enshrined as the precondition for all authentic selfhood, Eigensinn. Hopefully Dylan will continue to remain

---

22   "Well, What Have We Here?", Jules Siegel, *Saturday Evening Post* (1966), rpt. in *Retrospective*, p. 160.

true to himself, in whatever directions it may lead him. Despite all the money that has come his way, I don't think he has sold out to the Bitch Goddess, Success. But why worry about the future, dear landlords, when the prince has already given us so much for the present? Or as the singer of "Oh, Sister" has it, "Time is an ocean but it ends at the shore / You may not see me tomorrow."

Made in the USA
San Bernardino, CA
15 September 2015